PLEASE DON'T BOMB THE GHOST OF MY BROTHER

ALSO BY JULIAN STANNARD

Rina's War (Peterloo Poets, 2001)
The Red Zone (Peterloo Poets, 2007)
The Parrots of Villa Gruber Discover Lapis Lazuli (Salmon Poetry, 2011)
The Street of Perfect Love (Worple Press, 2014)
What were you thinking? (CB Editions, 2016)
Sottoripa: Genoese Poems (Canneto Editore, 2018)
Average is the New Fantastico (Green Bottle Press, 2019)
Heat Wave (Salt, 2020)

JULIAN STANNARD

Please Don't Bomb the Ghost of My Brother

CROMER

PUBLISHED BY SALT PUBLISHING 2023

2 4 6 8 10 9 7 5 3

First published in Great Britain in 2023 by
Salt Publishing Ltd
12 Norwich Road, Cromer, Norfolk NR27 0AX United Kingdom

www.saltpublishing.com

Salt Publishing Limited Reg. No. 5293401

A CIP catalogue record for this book is available from the British Library

ISBN 978 1 78463 306 6 (Paperback edition)

Typeset in Sabon by Salt Publishing

Printed and bound in Great Britain by Clays Ltd, Elcograf S.p.A

For Jack and William and
in loving memory of my brother

'I'm not in the mood for all this today. I have no desire to demonstrate, surprise, amuse, or persuade. My goal is absolute rest. To know nothing, to teach nothing, to want nothing, to sense nothing, to sleep, and then to sleep more.'

CHARLES BAUDELAIRE.

Contents

PLEASE DON'T BOMB THE GHOST OF MY BROTHER

Confessio Amantis

I like to row along the river,
a quiet moment with myself,
the oars dip in, the oars slip out.

You can imagine can't you
how I felt when under wave
and under gull I saw the barge
break through the mist –
I saw King Richard clear as day
standing there in pointed shoes
and wrapped, it seemed,
in damask cloth. I'd like to say

something eglantine
had spread across the day
but blood, I think, had fired my wit.
Is that John Gower? he said.
Yes sire, I mumbled, fiddling
somewhat with my oars.
Going rather fast? he said.
Poet, you'd better climb aboard!

Shit, I whispered to myself
though quickly I switched to *merde*.
I'm all scuffed up and haven't
trimmed my beard and had, in truth,
been feeling somewhat windy
since eating peas in Eastcheap.
A poet's lunch! And Richard
not one to be displeased, at least

not yet, and not a king with whom
one blows in easy ways.

I stood with Richard on the barge,
my feet seemed very small indeed.
We looked at spire and bridge
and smoke and Richard said,
giving me a nudge, My city is like?
All eyes upon me now.
Majesty, your city is like, your city
is like, that's it, your city is like
a patient etherised upon a table!

There was a gasp of course,
the lords all twitched and grasped
their doublets, I saw the river
cruel and deep, I turned to see
the ravens on the Tower but Richard
said, Oh Gower, most excellently
done! And, as if not to be usurped,
his pointed shoes tapping out
a pleasing rhythm, his royal palms
towards the sky, the great king said

Boneless Leg of Lamb Slow Cook Recipe

31 Dec 2019

There's something happening to my head.
(Thank you for Travelling in the Underworld said the notice
which I must have misread.)
This is the Piccadilly Line to Cockfosters.

I see the reflection of myself in the window.
The top of my head's gone crazy and the upside-down version
is pushing from above. Arsenal, Turnpike Lane . . .

Arse for Art's Sake!

I'm becoming the twice of me, I don't like it much.
I'm a Siamese twin on the line to Cockfosters.
I'm two for the price of one. I need another head
to make a Trinity. *It's not yesterday anymore . . .*

Everyone's making an effort. Bow-ties and Coco Chanel
and laundered underpants, dressing up for the doctor.
The red on the white, the blood on the snow,
the old hokey pokey. All the better to stick you with.

Think of London, a small city, dark in the daytime –

I'm at the table, a long table. I have to finish the pudding.
The garden hovered outside the window and there were the voices
of children and there were birds. I can't remember the birds.
A clock on the wall ticked, ticked, and my mother was saying
You can sit there till you've finished the whole lot.

I picked up the bowl of rice pudding
and hurled it through the window
and because the summer was golden
it sailed through the window in slow motion –

Oh! Oh! Oh! You should have seen my mother's face.

The revolution won't be televised.
Only a bowl of rice in slow motion.

I found no pleasure in the Pleasure Gardens.
Someone's eating a bowl of sweat
and the man in the blazer
has the letters L-O-V-E tattooed on his left hand.

Australia's burning.

China's cooking something up
in a Leviathan wok.

Love in the Time of Corona

Lockdown, the sails hunger for a wind.
Violins in the rafters. In the middle flat Ella Fitzgerald sings
Clams do it, oysters do it, jellyfish do it.

The love microbe slips off its bathrobe.

Be not afeard. The house is full of noises.
Sounds that wake you in the night.
Beds and sofas pull up anchor. Headboards
bang on walls. Sheets hang from windows,
salty sails for a tailwind.
Lazarus foreshadowed the resurrection.
The blonde goes down on the boy's erection.

The crow's nest sways.
The Bulgarians set up post-communist love regimes.
Such energy.
The house judders and swoons and moans.

I look at the moon
because the moon loves being looked at.

On dry land there is no touch. Touchless.
Daily bulletins of the dead.

In this house molluscs and cracked ceilings.
Neighbours crack each other open.
I watch a film about O. J. Simpson's glove.

We've become Wilhelm Reich's Orgone Energy Accumulator,

Model 2.
The gasket blows in the engine room.

Notes are slipped under my door.
One says Don't be the asshole on the Good Ship Lollipop.

One says I love you baby.

One night my door is knocked upon.
I open it an inch and see the platinum girl.
Her lips have kissed so much
they're puffed up like a boxer's.

We have no sugar in the crow's nest captain.
I fill her cup with sugar. I give her sugar:

slave sugar   love sugar   sugar-sugar.

Zoom Time

I

One of the most wretched things about lockdown
was being zoomed into hundreds of well-lit
middle class homes whose impeccable taste
made me feel down at heel, even shitty,
as if I were Edward Lear sitting at the table of Lord Stanley
trying to make the soup not trickle into my beard
and called upon at any moment to entertain (a singular fellow.)

There was an Old Person of Cromer who stood on one leg
reading Homer . . .

2

Artfully arranged bookshelves frame the background
of every zoomer, the libraries of the baby boomer –
Sometimes I catch the titles on the spines: Proudhon,
The 120 Days of Sodom, Plato's critique of humour.

3

The undoubted advantage of a zoom conference,
as far as I can tell, is that no one
has banned smoking although I have to admit
that when I took out a cigarette which I did
without thinking, I am after all sitting in my room,
not book-lined but nevertheless containing
an impressive collection of revolving ashtrays,
so as to lift the familiar stick to my wanting lips,

I understood I was smoking in the face
of a global plague and suddenly I was afraid.

4

The don from Cambridge is explaining that the poem
he is about to read, I fear it won't be short,
required the reading of one thousand five hundred books.
I suspect behind him in that donnish room
we can see the one thousand five hundred books.

5

Oh fellow zoomers
how much lovelier to think of a theatre
playing THE SHOW CAN'T GO ON!

An empty stage with blood-red seats
and balconies with strips of gold.

A man is walking across the stage.
He stops and turns and smiles.
Very old school, *Ja*, he says.

You think life disappointing?
We have no troubles here! Here life is beautiful.
The girls are beautiful, the orchestra is beautiful.
And for a tantalising moment we can see the girls
and hear the orchestra,
like the shadow of a coachman outside a hermitage.

Death – please – thou shalt die.

6

There's a young couple in one of the boxes
sitting entwined in comfortable repose.
The man's hand is on the woman's knee
and I'm wondering what would happen
if, in the comfort of their sitting room,
they forget that in panoptic mode
fifty pairs of eyes can see how
knee touching leads to greater acts
of intimacy; their caresses more ardent,
more urgent – O Corinna, Corona!
Someone has turned up the wattage,
some unexpected zoomer frottage . . .

7

I notice the professor from St Petersburg
has left his chair and I lean forward to see
if I can make out any titles in that august language.
He has several shelves of Gogol
(for a fleeting moment I thought he had the tales
of Nikolai Vasilyevich Google)
which brings me a sudden unbridled joy.
I too will leave my place, if only to return,
like Banquo at the feast of Zoom –
and let the viewers admire my wall of nothing,

I saw the shadow of a coachman
who with the shadow of a brush
did clean the shadow of a coach

Bird Mother

Easter 2020

My mother's ninety-one, she's in the garden,
nuts for the bird box, biscuits for the dog.
I sent her an Easter card, with an elephant.
The Easter Elephant. A hundred rabbits don't make a horse,
a hundred rabbits don't make an elephant.

Rabbits scatter on the heath.
They're listening to Ella Fitzgerald on tiny earphones.
Birds do it, fleas do it, bees do it,
even Pekineses in the Ritz do it, and Oh yes!
the rabbits shout together, we do it.

Let's absolutely fall in love.

Blue tits zoom to the nut box.
There's a robin which comes into the kitchen mother says.
It flies through the house and out the front door
leaving shit bombs on the wall. You think it's the same robin?
It has a routine – it hops into the kitchen, looks at me
as if to say – and off through the house and out the front . . .

There're lots of robins I guess.
What's that? Mother's fiddling with her hearing aid.
Electronic vibrations pulse down the phone.

Her garden's full of birds and dogs buried under the sycamore tree
and a one-eyed cat called Nellie. She was nineteen.
My father was cremated. His ashes scattered under the tree.
My brother was lost at sea.

Mother says
I dreamt mother was knocking.
I couldn't get myself up so I shouted out
Don't worry, Julian will open the door.

Mother, I'm hundreds of miles away.

Because from time to time
she uses father's hearing aid,
(now he has no use for it)
his voice comes down the line.
I can hear you clear as a bell.
How's that old dog of mine?
Oh daddy there were so many.
They're all sleeping under the tree.

Yesterday, mother says, the robin didn't come.
It was a fine day, all the doors and windows open.
There was a robin at the bird box
but it wasn't mine, I managed to look.
Perhaps it will come tomorrow, I say –

I had another visitor.
Her voice is weaving around the electronic vibrations.
It was a song thrush, got into the hallway.
It was petrified. I took it in my hands.
It was beautiful.
I stepped into the garden and set it free.

Keep Two metres Apart, Save Lives, It Said

at the entrance to the graveyard.
Dear dead people you should relax,
turn a blind eye, two blind eyes
if you prefer. I would advise you
to shake your bones and disinter.

Lean over to a corpse

in ectoplasmic ecstasy.

Now that you are dead you're safe!

Dear safe dead people
a large man in white gloves is standing
in the middle of the graveyard,
singing *Nessun Dorma! Nessun Dorma!*

He's scattering rose petals here and there.

Dear dead people,
I would urge the letting down of your hair.

Consider that pre-Raphaelite beauty
whose fiery curls blossomed and bloomed
filling the coffin after death.

The worms agog.

An endless plate of perfectly cooked
and freshly seasoned Spaghetti Alle Rossetti.

The dead, the un-dead, the half-dead –
The determinedly-doggedly- dead –
The occasional – Hardyesque – dog head –

Huggermugger.

And when I walk home late
through the graveyard
I will not complain
if an arm reaches out
and grabs me by the leg.

Radio Requests

I lost last year my wife of fifty years, sweet Mavis.
Would you, could you play some Miles Davis?

My partner's gotten Alzheimer's.
The days have shrunk.
Spread some joy with Thelonious Monk.

I lost my father, the days are darker.
Could you play some Charlie Parker?

I kicked my addiction to cocaine.
If you could play anything by John Coltrane
I'd open another bottle of champagne.

A kumquat for a quintet.
A jazz band in a dream land!

I switched gender. I call myself Cherry.
I'd dance across the room if you played Chuck Berry.

Last year was a train wreck.
Time, surely, for Dave Brubeck.

The days are grey, the sky is gloopy.
Energise us with Fela Kuti.

Last year my husband was so unkind
I ran away.
Could you play something by Billie Holiday?

I popped the question to my girlfriend Jean.
A thumbs up!
We're gagging for some Bunky Green.

My auntie's knitting Kashmiri shawls.
A sudden blast of Biggie Smalls?

After thirty years of marriage
my wife threw in the towel –
(leaping off a bridge) –
Oh Maisy! Maisy! Maisy!
She was always partial to Count Basie.

Shall we, shan't we, should we, let's.
Give us something by Stan Getz.

This year I gave birth to Jerome.
Almost anything please by Nina Simone!

It was our first wedding anniversary last year
(I don't normally tell people this,
I met my husband at Walmart . . .)
We lowered the blinds,
a tip-top afternoon with Django Reinhart.
Would you? Could you? Should you?

I grabbed it online and paid the acquisition fee!
Bring on the trumpets, Dizzy Gillespie.

I recently qualified as a Level Two Undertaker.
Please play My Funny Valentine by Chet Baker.

We lost dear Max on Boxing Day.
Our loving selfless Dachshund dog.
Could we hear the voice of Karin Krog?

My dentist went completely mad
and pulled out all my teeth.
I now make a weird sucking noise
which goes quite well with 'Tootie' Heath.

Last year I had a stroke.
I would like to listen to some Elmo Hope.

Last year another breakdown, I was sent away . . .
Reel me back with Sidney Bechet.

A kumquat for a quintet.
A jazz band in a dream land!

Last month I gave up and laid down
for the last time my weary head.
Could you play The Grateful Dead?

Duck Corner

I'll meet you at Duck Corner.

                    I'll be riding Gauloises
my newly acquired horse.

He used to clop along
Boulevard Saint-Michel
singing *Le Monde Entier Fait Boum!*

with Simone de Beauvoir
and Jean-Paul Sartre.

Of course –

Now it's Duck Corner . . .

In fact the only person who isn't there
is you!

I like it when you're late.
Even better when you're dead –

So déjà vu.
I should be stricken by remorse.

If my mouth could open wider
I'd smoke the entire horse.

Have you noticed
our meetings at Duck Corner never work out?

The hooves of the horse are hoofing.
It's so wretchedly déjà vu.

Have you read *The Magnificent Smoking Horse*
by Albert Camus?

Better Now Or Better Now Or Better Never?

Can you put your chin on the rest please. Super.
Look straight ahead into the light, if you can see the light.
Can you see the light? I didn't think you could.
If it makes you feel better 90 percent of my patients
can see the light. You'll have to imagine the light.
Can you look to the left? To the right. Look up, look down.
And now straight ahead. Super. You can sit back now.
Would you like a mint?

I'm going to put some drops in your eyes.
Might sting a bit. Look up. Super. Again. Super.
Can you read any of the letters on the chart?
I didn't think so. If it makes you feel better
90 percent of my patients can read the first two rows.
Can you put your chin back on the rest. Super.
Look straight ahead into the light you cannot see
and when the orange mist lifts you'll notice a road
which appears to be leading to eternity.

Can you see the long road which appears
to be leading to eternity? Yes I can actually. I can.
Beautiful. Does it remind you of that song
by Talking Heads, We're on the road to nowhere?
Super. Keep looking down that long road.
Is it clearer now, or now? Is it clearer now, or now?
Or the same? The same. No – clearer now.
I can see a balloon. You can see a balloon?

Beautiful. Look closely at the balloon and tell me
whether you can see a person in a wicker basket.

You might like to think of the 1870 siege of Paris,
the Prussians are at the gates, elephant soup
is on the menu, the French are climbing into balloons,
trying to flee. Can you see anyone in the wicker basket?

I can see someone in the wicker basket. Can you tell me
who that person is? It's rather blurred. Of course.
If it makes you feel better 80 percent of my patients
only see a balloon and have never heard of
the Franco-Prussian War and would not be having
this conversation. Wicker basket my arse . . .

Better now, or now, or now, or never?
Try again, better now, or now? Better now.
Beautiful. Are you able to tell me who the person
in the wicker basket is? Strange as it may sound
I think it's Priti Patel. Well, well, well
it *is* Priti Patel! You can sit back now.

There's a knock at the door.
The ophthalmologist's assistant comes in with a note.
She gives it to him and slips out. Did you notice anything
unusual about my assistant? She was somewhat blurred.
Of course she was. He calls out a name and
the assistant comes back. Is she clearer now, or now?
Clearer now? Or the same? Clearer now. Super –

Let me ask you again, did you notice anything unusual?
Yes, she looks like Priti Patel! Doesn't she just!
Would you like another mint?

I've examined your retinal scans.
I'm sorry to say you have an eye disease
called Priti-Patelitis. It's quite serious.
We need to check out its rate of progress.
If we diagnose early we might be able to slow it down.
You're still likely to have unpleasant side effects.
Have to live with it I'm afraid.

Can you put your chin back on the rest. Super.
And could you hold this hand pump
in your right hand. Super-duper.
We're going to watch an optic video simulator
called Corneal Protection Level Three.

Look at the long road which appears to be
going absolutely nowhere and when you hear the beep
you'll find your plane of vision inundated
with microscopic Patels, some striding out
of Whitehall looking smug, some marching
through Jerusalem with members of the Likud,
some leaping up and down like Rumple what's his name.

As the eye pressure increases
a miniature Patel will seek to penetrate
your nasolacrimal duct
and push into the hippocampus.

Try and zap Home Secretary Patel
the bat out of hell
by squeezing the hand pump.

Are you ready?

Beautiful. You can sit back now.
Shot of brandy?
Might as well enjoy things whilst you can.

He calls for his assistant.
Could you run these off please. Beautiful.
We'll have the results in twenty minutes.
Do you mind if we listen to some Ravel?

Buttocks

In the autumn of 1967 a cloud in the shape of
human buttocks appeared over Krakow
NINA FITZPATRICK

A pair of buttocks forging along Shirley High Street
without feet, legs, arms, without anything –

Only when Adeline tried to sit down
did she realise something was wrong.

Too late now.

She shouldn't have spent so much time
on TikTok. She shouldn't have abandoned
Russian literature.

Cut me some slack, the buttocks said
and made a dash for it.
A magnificently large pair of buttocks
with no little swag.
They were going for Egalité, Fraternité and Liberté.
They wanted to sing La Marseillaise.
They couldn't remember the words.

The buttocks drop into Boots
and buy some Coco Mademoiselle.
They make their way down Shirley High Street
in a vapoury halo of lime and patchouli.

Workmen high in the sky with hard hats
whistle so hard
their teeth hurtle across the city.

A small but growing number of youths
start following.
What a day!
The pied piper of buttocks
swinging their way down Shirley High Street.

Jouissance!

They pass the Pie Shop. Nice.
And the Pawn shop.
Nothing to pawn. Only denim
made in that faraway country
EL-AL Chutzpah.

The buttocks nip into the Black Sea Supermarket.
Welcome, welcome,
when it comes to goats and/or buttocks
there's no discrimination here.
They pop some Bulgarian goat cheese
into a back pocket.

The buttocks pass the Turkish Barber's
and the barbers say
Come in! Come in!
I have no hair to cut my lovelies
Come in anyway, *please* . . .

We could do a head massage.
You couldn't, you couldn't.

They sail past the Bingo Hall and the Catholic church
and there's the beginning of a traffic jam
and the hooting
of horns but the buttocks are unconcerned
and move with purpose and panache.
They cross the road
and wave to the held-up cars.
They're waving without hands.

The buttocks make their way
to the local library
which is next to Lidl.
They ordered a book a long time ago.

Where on earth are we?
says one of the men.
Shit happens says another.
The librarians smile,
an unusual occurrence.

Why not borrow some crime fiction,
the unofficial biography of Prince Andrew?
Why not borrow fantasy? People love fantasy.
No, the buttocks say, we want something by Gogol.
Who? they say.

Google it!

The book has arrived
and now the buttocks are collecting it.
It had taken the library a long time
to track Gogol down who was happy
not to be tracked down
but they tracked him down.
Now the buttocks are going
to take him on a road trip
and they leave the library
with some Bulgarian goat cheese
in one pocket and Gogol in the other.

If one pair of buttocks weren't enough
on the other side of the road
going in the opposite direction
there's another.

These are wearing football shorts.
They were tired of losing matches
and just as Alfie was taking a shower
they said Oh no what's that over there?
Where? *There!* And when
he turned
the buttocks ducked and shimmied,
patted themselves down
with a towel, threw on a pair
of clean shorts and legged it
(without legs of course)
down Cawte Road.

If one were preparing
a spreadsheet of buttocks
these would go in a different column.

As if Aphrodite had called on Polykleitos of Argos
saying, I don't want common-or-garden buttocks.
I want buttocks which sail through
the theatre of Dionysius like a chariot of fire –
I want buttocks which shimmer
in the bathhouse like the sun rising over the hill.
I want buttocks which give Tom of Finland
a run for his money.

These buttocks aren't without followers either:
women, men and a three-legged Golden Retriever.

People are opening their windows
and playing that old game lobbing the nut.

(Any nut will do –)

If they hit the spot the buttocks crack them.
Crack! Crack! *Crack!* left right and centre
as if they were setting off firecrackers
in the back streets of Naples
as if they were at the Festival of San Gennaro
waiting for blood.

The buttocks slip into the Misty Magic Tattoo Parlour.
India says I have been waiting for you

and the buttocks begin their lamentation:
Alfie has tattoos
on his arms and legs and chest and thighs
and we're a tabula rasa.

India wanted to put an arm round their shoulder.
There weren't any shoulders.

It is what it is India said.
They are what they are.

Move over Michelangelo, these are mine.
Shall we do the elephant god on one,
and Lord Shiva on the other?

The buttocks slip back into their shorts
throbbing paradoxically.

The buttocks in denim head for the Pig 'N Whistle.
The others are heading for the hinterland.

There's a choice.

Oh no, Oh no
choice
is
despair!

A Bobby Dazzler for Alan Brownjohn

Although I won't be there for your party
it makes me feel good to think of those times
you turned up in a suit
which was always magnificently classy.

You were the poet who dazzled and shone.
In fact there wasn't anyone
who ever managed to look so cool and arty.

It's your ninetieth birthday party.
I'd like to sing an old-fashioned song.
I've brought my lyre and I've brought my lute.

Here's hoping you'll have umpteen more occasions
to be a tad dissolute.

We can't wait to see you in your birthday suit.

A Gash in Your Head

What if
you thought you could tie your laces?
But all this time you were just wrapping
a whole roll of sellotape round your shoe and
hoping for the best?

CAROLINE BIRD

You walk through the city
with a gash in your head.
The crowds part like the Red Sea.
The blood drips on the pavement.
Someone takes a picture
and puts it on social media.
Oh DADA is back, they say.

Did DADA ever go away?

You walk through the city
with your heart on your sleeve.
Heart doesn't look good
nor does the sleeve.
You need psychosurgery,
several therapy dogs . . .
No one hangs about.
The only dog in town savages your foot.

You walk through the city
with an eviction notice.
In the grand scheme of things
it's not a great deal of money.

You don't have any money.
You rely on the kindness of strangers.

The crowds part like the Red Sea.
The homeless man follows you
up and down the street
assiduously.

You walk through the city
with your shoelace undone.
The whole city stops and trembles.
The city has not one visceral clutch

but two.

Your friendly dealer puts an arm around you
like a brother.
Mate, he says, I'm not your mother.
I have to warn you about that lace.
It's a disgrace. It's out of order: it's undone.
You happen to know your friendly dealer
carries a gun.

The bus driver stops his bus
opens a window and shouts
Oi, your lace is undone!

You try and look grateful.
You look sheepish.

So many people on the case.
They want you to bend over
and rectify the situation
without hesitation

The Kray Twins appear.
Footwear impeccable.

On a good day
Ronnie can put his nose in the air
and pluck out that smell in Ravel.

Don't mind us Sonny Jim.
You want a lump of ice?
You could do yourself an injury
What with that lace of yours.
You need to take care of yourself,
What with that lace of yours.

You don't want to bend over
in front of Ronnie
there on the street
arse
sticking out –

You need to find a low wall,
a bench –
you need a little space
a little privacy.
You don't want to tie your lace

in front of the whole city
watching and waiting and trembling

You walk on.

The country's run by liars and crooks.
Across the planet there are wars going on.
There's famine and starvation.
You guess the city's losing interest in your lace.

About time.

A convent of nuns crosses the road.
They're following Sister Marie
and Sister Marie is following you.

The city was having a breather.

You're in the clutches of nuns.
Sisters of Rectitude
Brides of Christ
Sister Marie blesses you –
she says
You don't want to fall over
and have yourself another gash.

Oh my child.

A novice bends
and ties the lace.

Partake of the sacraments
says Sister Marie
and swirls off into the city.

Now your lace is tied
the crowds part like the Red Sea.
You almost have the city to yourself.
You feel skittish
and embark on a little tap dancing
with a gash in your head.

The blood drips on the pavement.
Someone takes a picture
and puts it on social media.
DADA is back, they say.

Did DADA ever go away?

You don't realise the other lace
is unravelling.

Ronnie puts his nose in the air.

Colonel Crust is wearing jodhpurs.
He's a decorated soldier
with a Rogan Josh on his left shoulder.
He waves his stick at you.

Men with shaved heads and necks
covered in tattoos who are capable
of violence are fretting.

Pope Innocent X appears
with a packet of Marlboro.
His boots are beautiful.
He smells a little of the Tiber.
His English is so-so-so.

I'm much concernèd about your shoe.
La scarpa, la scarpa.
You stoop and kiss his ringed finger.
He doesn't linger.

You imagined he'd performed a miracle
that the lace had tied itself
so although you were blessed
you were nevertheless undone.

The Kray Twins
are getting hot under the collar.
Yves Saint Laurent appears
as does Jimmy Choo.
In Stoke Newington
you lie down in the beautiful arms
of a beautiful Jew.

The Crossing

The lone stag's crossing a field.
He's done with rutting.
Outside Snape Maltings
he listens to Alexander Gadjiev.
He's got Chopin in his head.
He misses the girls.
He's missing an antler.
The sky is blood-red.
The sonata was perfect.

He's always had a thing
about New York.
He slips into the water
at Bawdsey.
His wounds are cauterised.
He's swimming
to Old Felixstowe.

He curls up in the bowels
of the ship
like Rimbaud.
He's not sure how things will go.
The stowaway stag.
He's going to start again.
He'd like some music.
He'd like to play the cello.
He'd really like a cigar.

Escalator City

Last month you'd never heard of it –
Now you're there hook, line and sinker
stepping onto an escalator
which is going up and up and up
the sunlight streaking your face –

and sometimes – what longing – you glimpse a city
(a real city) Berlin, Athens, London, Budapest, Rome.

Weren't you glad when you reached
the gates of Hyderabad?

Now you're rising
and then, as if it were a game
of snakes and ladders,
you're going down . . .

A moment of reflection – oh no, not that – *reflection!*

One moment you're up like a Tiramisu.
The next you're going down like a plum pudding.

By the way
it's not the sort of place you can get away from in a hurry.

There was, I think, an entrance –

Welcome.

We Appreciate Slow –Walkers, Non-Talkers
and – please note – Staring Is Forbidden!

No point running up the escalator
because you imagined you saw something
plucked from the world – a white horse say,
a house with a garden and some befuddled shed.
Saying shed makes you feel giddy.

Shed, shed –giddy – giddy – oh!

Some people are sent to Escalator City
as a punishment – *I did something wrong.*

No one used to lie in bed saying:
Please don't send me to Escalator City.
I'd rather shove a stick in my eye.

You've been sentenced to a month in Escalator City.
Oh weep for me.
You've been sentenced to six months.
Oh weep for me even more
Up and up, in search of redemption.
The city on the hill with moving walkways –

Tiramisu with whips!

Some come to Escalator City for therapy.
The rhythms of ascent (Apotheosis)

and descent (Gehenna) etc etc will nudge
the frontal cortex into the right position
and have an improving effect
on the buttocks – a cosmic re-alignment.
Two months of therapeutic escalators
and you will step into the horizontal world
like an evangelical toaster.

You will be new – like a wedding gift.

A walking miracle.

Sometimes the warmest aromatic winds
greet you on the escalator
and your private parts buzz with satisfaction.
On those occasions the escalators
are full of tantalising opportunities.
The next escalator sends an Arctic wind
which stops you in your tracks.
Oh Lord Shiva what have I done?
Have I not suffered enough?
I'm afraid not, there's always more to come.
The steps of the escalator
are onto you like the teeth of a shark.

There are more announcements:
Escalators are moving pieces of machinery.
Please hold onto the handrail.
Please do not stare – don't fall asleep.
No kissing, no horse play – no horses.

No inappropriate touching.
Please be aware you are about to step off
the escalator – there will be a jolt
as if you were about to leap off a turret.
No turret to leap off – concentrate.
See it, say it, shag it (shag what?)
Escalator City would seem a shagless kind of place.
Sometimes a pigeon zips through.
Sometimes music.
The least interesting songs of Steely Dan.
Some days everybody looks like Bamber Gascoigne.
Sometimes an advert – Are you feeling tired?

Yes!

There are walkways between the escalators
and designated food stations
where they serve durian fruit
and beef cheek with pearl barley (Paul Bailey?)
and reconstituted cattle burgers,
whose gherkins were consecrated by the pope.

And there are lavatorial breaks which are,
without doubt, the most agreeable thing.
Your buttocks are washed with kumquat spray
and dried to perfection by a Kyoto breeze.
You look forward to your next evacuation.
(Montaigne was fond of his bowels.)
The excrement is sucked into the oubliette
which goes down and down and down

to a state-of-the-art recycling plant
and which then climbs up and up and up
in a Nietzschean loop of everlastingness.

Thud

The blind boy had a lover
who was ravenous. A raven?
How would he know?
Her mouth hungry as a puppy
her arms so plucky, lucky.

He couldn't see whether
he was on the Inner Circle or the Outer.

He couldn't see the People's Palace.
He couldn't see Buchanan Street.
He couldn't see the Clyde.

He could hear the wind. He could hear the gulls.
He could hear the thud of a ball.
He could hear the chanting –
his lover tied herself to his foot
her hair was black of course.

NOX PERPETUA

He wanted to make a film. He enrolled on a course:
Federico Fellini, Rosselini, Bolognini, Pasolini
and Stevie Wonder rolled into one.

The *mise-en-abyme*, the universal scream.
He was interrogating the existential hole
not some cameo role –

He hatched a plan and flipped a fugue.
Break into the Kelvingrove Gallery
under the cover of night, perpetual night,
steal Dalí's Crucifixion.

No thorns, no blood, no nails
suspended above a lake –
ready to slide into the lake.

First they went to Mother India to eat –
to work out the ins and outs.
Kenny slapped a paratha
round his face, an instant balaclava.

Powder your face with sunshine.
Put on a great big smile . . .

They lowered Christ of Saint John of the Cross
onto the boy's back.
He had broad shoulders,
his calf muscles strengthened
by amorous trysts.

Tricky getting out of the door.

And he walked down Argyle Street
as if it were Palm Sunday
with sixty million pounds of Salvador Dalí
          on his back –

Tricky getting back into the flat
with Christ of Saint John of the Cross on his back –
The neighbours gawping.

But there's always a chance
with Christ on your back
of a MIRACOLO fast track.
The boy got his sight back!

Raven lay on her back, aflutter. Ecstatic boy.
He was the lead man in his own film.
He'd acquired the gift of sight.
He'd thumbed his nose at the police.
He'd escaped with the Crucifixion.
There was trouble, however, with his erection.

He clambered onto the raven
like a winged aardvark
heavy, locked in, soft –

No nails in his hands
Christ slid down the cross
into the lovers' bed.
A ménage a trois. A thud.

A kitsch triptych.

Imagine there's no heaven.
Quite easy if you try.

A short film –
it won several prizes.

L'Osservatore Romano
said it was shot through
with a slither of evil.

Who Stuffed Veronica Hackett?

My mother asked me to take a bag
of stuffing to my sister who lives
on the other side of the heath.

It was Christmas Eve and there was a large turkey
needing to be stuffed.
Don't speak to any strangers and if anyone leaps out
pretend you've alighted from your camel
that you're carrying some Coco-Frankensteen.

Now go, go, I've finished one bottle of gin
and I am about to start on another.

It was Christmas Eve and there was a large turkey
who would feel complete only when it was stuffed.
There were owls and foxes and mulch
and there was a bohemian hare with an Afghan coat
its ears pointing to the moon,
the wind going thither and hither.
It was the biggest bag of stuffing I had ever seen
a stuffing machine and notwithstanding the cold
it was frisky –

The only person I could imagine seeing on the heath
was Veronica Hackett.
Oh what are you carrying across the heath on Christmas Eve
in the dark?
An unimaginably large bag of stuffing, all the better to stuff you with.

There was a choir of rabbits huffing and puffing
singing Marxist carols that not without guile
referred to class war and the history of stuffing.
Bravo, bravo I said and they bowed.

The bag was growing and growing
and white crystals were falling from the sky
because it was Christmas and because it was snowing.
I mulched on in my Russian boots listening to the owl hoots.

At my sister's house on the other side of the heath
there was expectation.
They were drinking bottles and bottles and bottles of gin
to wash away the tang of original sin.
And the turkey alone in the kitchen was crooning:

If I should take a notion
to jump into the ocean
ain't nobody's business if I do –

If I go to church on Sunday
then cabaret all day Monday
ain't nobody's business if I do –

Suffolk Roulette

Christmas we drive to Rendlesham Forest.
Drinks with S and T.
Cars piled up on tracks.
A man on a white horse.
Some people do the Christmas wave.
The dogs mud splattered.

T loves old cars, now he thinks we're his –
rather than diesel he's giving us fizz.

The log fire spits. No one sits on the sofas.
The springs have sprung.
Last Christmas two men pulled mother up.

There are additions and subtractions:
wives, mistresses, dogs –
a son released from open prison.

The handsome middle-aged homosexual
arrives with a new friend – a Russian.
The yearly death toll, minor or major.

The 'general'– so called – isn't here this year.
Manoeuvres in Elysium.
He made his fortune in Mongolia.

There's a red-faced colonel
who did something hush-hush in Bulgaria,
with a roving eye
and an Irish wolfhound who gobbles up the canapés.

The dogs huddle by the fire
smelling of horse shit.

This is a house with many rooms.
S is in the kitchen, with handfuls of salmon.
The Aga, as always, plotting.

Someone wanders into the attic,
plays Suffolk roulette.

The gardener clomps down the stairs
smelling of weed.

He lets the garden do its own thing.
Knows where the dogs are buried.

H the heroin addict
inherited a fortune and lost it all.
He's wearing a blazer and is on the dole.
Munching a smoked oyster.

Men in herbaceous jackets.
Camouflage.
The women tweedy and pearled.
Each face an anatomical adventure,
a glamorous disaster.
Wedding cakes left out in the rain
and for good measure left out again.

Happy Christmas!
S and T have turned on the green light.
V says, Oh I'm half cut!

An oyster catcher flies over the house.
The deer appear.

It's beginning to rain.

D's grandfather governed
much of India.
D's a functioning alcoholic.
He's functioning well.
V says Got a fag darling?
She knew Lucien Freud.
Every year she tells me this.

The smokers tramp into the garden
and stand in a circle.
S waves from the window.

Summer Pudding

My mother gave me a summer pudding
to take to my sister
who lives on the other side of the heath.

Take it to the other side of the heath
without letting the juices spill
or the pudding drop.
Keep your arms out like so.

If Veronica tries to get the pudding
I'll shoot her from morning to noon
and then I'll shoot her from noon to midnight.

The gun's in the shed, oiled up and pumping.
Here, off you go, I have a bottle of gin
that's waiting to be drunk
and my fly swat's at the ready.

I walk across the heath which is full of ferns.
Green is the colour of the heath in summer
when the rain has fallen and the sun has shone.

There are swathes of purple
and hollyhocks and lad's love and rue
and sorrel and a couple of lesbians
with Great Danes.

A stag leaps out from behind a tree
and hundreds and hundreds of rabbit ears are twitching.
I'm halfway now, holding out the pudding
in its purple glory on a lovely plate.

(A long time ago
kings were crowned with summer puddings.

Ethelred the Unready are you ready?

Not quite.)

I know Veronica's out there somewhere
lurking dirty behind the ferns.
Full of scratches and itches.
The ground strewn with bottles
and the steaming shit of a horse
swarming with bug life.

I found her sleeping once:
Old Mole chewing her foot,
a copy of *Dead Souls*
a pillow for her head – almost happy.

I'm in sight of my sister's house
and Veronica's heathy breath
makes my ears tingle and my arms ache.

Ah the summer pudding she says.
I knew it was time.
All the summer fruits jostling at a débutante's party.
She's drooling like a dog.
Your débutante days are over, I say.

I've been waiting for it behind the ferns.
No Veronica, fuck off, you can't have it.
Oh but I will, I will and she's tugging at my trousers
and my sister's on the stoop shouting
Keep going! Keep going!
Veronica, please, I'm almost there.
She says, Me want that fecund pudding now.

Miss Lady Macbeth

Son of Charles flew to Belfast, hired a car
and drove to a farm where they sold him
a tiny dog. Tiny dog now back in London.
Shepherd's Bush if you please –

The dog was too tiny to leap onto the sofa
which somehow thwarts the reason for being a dog.
So Charles built a ramp, a tiny dog- to-sofa-ramp.

And that might have been the end of it
were it not for the fact that tiny is now the word
of the day, the word of the month and catching.

The two cats, small, are smaller now.
Lady Macbeth becoming Miss Lady Macbeth.
The mice laughed at her, tiny laughs if you will.

The books in Charles' house have begun to shrink:
pocketbooks, some the size of postage stamps.
The Brothers Karamazov a walnut whip.
Pop it in your mouth, won't have to read it now.

And the cigarettes so very tiny too.
You're smoking three packets a day
to keep your hand in.

Or lie there on the sofa saying Fuck it!
watching tiny dog climbing the ramp
and wondering if the wife's not shrinking too,
to fit in, tiny, why not?

Oh titchy tiny dog, let's call him Toni, *Toni Macaroni*
tiny barks, tiny licks of the ear, tiny tiny everything.

Jamaica Road

I walked down Jamaica Road in terrible rain.
Natalia and Jenny and Jack washed away.
An old lady pulled me to my feet
linking arms, helping me up and on –
and helping herself to my wallet.
What disappointment when she opens it.

After much Weialala leia   Wallala leialala
I fetched up in Charles' sitting room
in Shepherd's Bush – Oh green so green and wet
so wet is Shepherd's Bush this rain-soaked night
and many flights of stairs above me.

Once I slept at the top.
I was a midshipman in the crow's nest
watching Napoleon
making his way down Uxbridge Road
like a crab thermidor.

I was cat sitting.
I could hear the cats down in the kitchen murmuring
Feed us! Feed us!

The bedraggled having walked down Jamaica Road me
is reading *Notes Without A Text*,
four-legged Harold at my shoulder
(he's forgiven me . . .)

Charles is rewriting *The Brothers Karamazov*
upstairs somewhere

with a typewriter – clackety clack.
He's making such a racket.

He's taking out the padding
and focusing on the good bits
making sure each character has only one name
which they stick to, or at least try to.

What a slim publication it's going to be.

A couple's making out on the stoop.
Couldn't you use another stoop? I say.
We like this one.
But it's raining.
We like doing it in the rain.
You have a problem with that?

Well yes, well no,   oh   oh

I See

Madeleine has a room filled with dresses
which are covered in plastic
because when Lucian comes round
with the dog
the dog tries to eat them.

The dog's called Reggie.

I dreamt about you
Madeleine says.

In the dream you climb down the stairs
remove the plastic and start eating.
You have the tail of a dog
which you wag.
You wag it rather well.

That is peculiar I say
because I had a dream too.

In the dream
I wake on the top floor
and feel peckish.
If there'd been a horse's head
in my bed I would have eaten
much of it.

I climb down the stairs
enter the room of dresses
remove the plastic

put a napkin round my neck
and tuck in with gusto.

I remember quite clearly
that in the dream
I wanted to wag something
but I didn't have a tail.
I just imagined having a tail.
You must have seen an imaginary tail.

I see.

Hips and Haws

for Fleur

I'm in a garden in north London, the wind is blowing.
It's full of trees and weeds and Sweet Williams.

A single butterfly comes and goes.
There's a shaft of sunlight too, breaking through.

Don't make me go to the end of the garden.
The trees are full of poets, whispering behind the leaves.

Stanley Kunitz smiles and rakes the grass.

How did you get here Stanley? Blown over
by a westerly, he says. He wipes a hand and shrugs.
Death is cruel and death is beautiful. It's part of the story.
We always knew it would happen. Now it's happening.

Don't over think it. See it as a curtain call, the crowning encore.
You should congratulate yourself you didn't take your own life.
Plenty of good people have, he says.

Those who live for years, whose minds unravel, as they will –
their words are seed-hoards which burst and scatter
fetching up in gardens both imaginary and real –
like hipsters, hobos, freight hoppers, hips and haws.

He takes a cooking apple from the tree and lobs it to me.

I'm Afraid the Loan Advisor Won't Be Able to See You

I used to go to a salon in Winchester.
Three women, all their customers were men
most of whom walked through the door with
little hair in the first place. The radio sang
and there was an Irish greyhound which wandered
around. Sometimes it would lie down
and spread itself across the floor, hoping to trip
someone over. I learnt later the bitch was spayed.

They preferred cash but there was a machine
and Siobhan noticed it said Doctor on my card.
We've got a doctor in the house, she said.
I felt a fraud. I had a PhD in Poetry.
I thought they'd treat me better if I told the bank
I was a doctor and for a while they did.
Good morning doctor how can we help you?
We'd be happy to increase your overdraft facilities.
Later, when they saw my title didn't come
with a doctor's salary they changed their tune.
I'm afraid the loan advisor won't be able to see you.

Siobhan didn't need to know about my finances
and I didn't need to know her gynaecological history.
Soon I knew it all. The next time I visited the salon
she laid it out in the air, full of twists and turns
like Odysseus trying to get back to the island of Ithaca.
She didn't mind her colleagues, one of them chipped in,
the other popped out for a fag. Or the men
whose hair was being cut, who'd surrendered
to a *Weltschmerz* of their own. Quiet as the greyhound.

When Siobhan massaged my head I felt relaxed
but the clippers nicked my ear which woke me up
and had me say *Yes yes yes, I think you might be right . . .*
When I went to pay – after Siobhan had given the machine
a little shake – I tried my doctor's voice:
If I were you Siobhan, I'd take it easy for a day or two.

Six weeks later I called by for a trim.
Siobhan was looking happy and smelling good.
I took your advice Doctor and it worked a treat.
Her colleagues said We sent her home, a week –
she came back like a bottle of Lucozade.

Siobhan massaged my head longer this time.
I was on the verge of sleep, deep sleep
then she got the clippers out.

If I were a real doctor –
a liver, heart and kidney doctor
an ears and throat doctor and would you cough doctor?
a little louder doctor.
Why are you putting on that glove doctor?
I'm going to put a finger in your rectum doctor,
it might be a slightly uncomfortable doctor.
Might it be the prostate doctor?
Would you touch your toes doctor? Now doctor?
If I were a real bread and butter doctor
I'd call myself Doctor Lambert.

Doctor Lambert is ready to see you now
and I'm ready to see Doctor Lambert.
There are photographs of his wife and children,
his shirt ironed to perfection.
And there's a framed certificate on the wall
to show he's a top-notch bona fide doctor.
And such a pleasant bedside manner.
When he looks at my notes
he does that twirling pen thing with his fingers.
Do you smoke? Once in a blue moon.
He winces like a priest. I want to listen to your heart.
I'm a listening to your heart doctor.
I'm a would you take your shirt off doctor.
I'm a come- and-see-me- if- you- have-concerns doctor.

Oh Doctor Lambert I have concerns.

The next time I visit Doctor Lambert
I get a butler's uniform from Moss Brothers.
I think Doctor Lambert deserves a butler.
Good morning Doctor Lambert. Good morning!
He has an air about him. He locks the door
and kicks his shoes off and takes a silver packet
from his drawer and leans over and offers me
a cigarette. There's one already peeping out,
– the alpha smoke – ready for some action.
He takes a zip lighter and leans across and
brings the cigarette to life, a short life.

He takes one from the packet, throws it in the air
and catches it in his mouth. I lean across
like a butler, I am a butler, and light his cig.
No photographs on the doctor's packet.
He sits back and puts his feet across the desk.

Once upon a time there was a Gorgonzola he says –
We exhale our beams of smoke across the room
like mini rockets launched from a microscopic launching pad
at the John F. Kennedy Space and Tobacco Center.
Titchy, I believe, is today's special word –

Doctor Lambert's shrinking, he's become a figurine.
a Lilliputian doctor with Lilliputian latex gloves
standing on his own desk.
His bedside manner remains impeccable.
He's trying out some titchy-tiny dance moves.
Who let the dogs out?

Not A City But A Beautiful Catastrophe

Nice sitting in Bar Barracuda in the Sottoripa
under the porticos, watching the city
come to life: the fish stalls, the hum
of the sopraelevata, the early-rising priests,
the cupola of Santa Maria delle Vigne
floating in vapour, the addicts, the hustlers,
the pimps, the street sellers, the matelots,
the fish-fryers, an endless unveiling
of gestures, and the Irishman
standing on his tower in Caricamento.
By eight o'clock the sun's broken through.
It's going to be a long, long day.

Piazza Della Lepre

There's a black door
in Piazza Della Lepre
with neoclassical figures.
The stairs lead up to a knocking shop,
at the very top.
The best in the city, oh what ceilings!
There's no lift.
You must walk up the slate stairs.
The stairs are steep.
Not everyone can:
heart seizure, ennui, brain softening
and some who do
never put their nose in the piazza again,
extinguished – it would seem – by rapture.
Number 9, Piazza Della Lepre.
Books have been written
and songs have been sung.
Any man of that age
would have taken their pleasure there
back in the day.
They were young.
They didn't walk up the stairs.
They – more or less – ran.

Goffredo Miglietta – Professor of English

In Memoriam

I heard Goffredo speak English only once.
At a lunch in honour of George MacBeth
who was reading at the Faculty.
He'd written *The Cleaver Garden*
which had a picture of a carcass on the front.
In the 1980s George was something of a star.
(MacBeth's dead now, motor neurone disease.)
Tomorrow and tomorrow and tomorrow . . .
Goffredo's slipped away in a Moroccan hat:
part of the great throng in the Bay of Silence.

George was married to Lisa St Aubin de Terán
who wrote *The Bay of Silence*
and later when they split up George wrote
Anatomy of a Divorce
and when I look at the table next to my bed
I can see *The Anatomy of Melancholy.*

There was no melancholy at the restaurant.
Goffredo became Chief Explainer of the Menu.
When it comes to the pasta George
there is – as we say – *un imbarazzo della scelta.*
You might try trenette with Ligurian pesto.
Why not plump for pansoti
which comes with sugo di noci, a walnut sauce?
Or the heavenly corzetti, which I'd recommend.
And if you're feeling, how should I say, vexed
you could always go for the pasta arrabbiata!
How will you nail your colours? Great MacBeth.

All eyes were on the poet now.
George – son of a Scottish miner – said
I don't like pasta.
(One might have thought
he'd stabbed Goffredo with an artichoke!)
However I do like watching people eat it.

Miracle in Lorsica

Dogs bark across the valley.
How's it going over there? Same old.
I ate some pickled walnuts.

I had the dregs of a minestrone
and a lousy fish head.
Lorenzo beat me with a stick.

Oh. You should come over here. I know.
Separated by a valley. It's tragico!

Bark bark bark.
Night-time, but not so dark.
The moon's beaming.
Mozzarellas ricochet across the sky.

I am agog –
although I haven't been to church for years
I see these angels.

Trainee angels, a touch piquant.
I guess they'd just been given their wings.
Having the time of their lives,
not much theological focus.
I'm not some crazed poet on bennies.

I saw those angels . . .

Mistress

Sestri Levante

I arranged to meet Gloria at the Gran Caffè Tritone.
I knew she'd be late so I drank a coffee and waited.
She was sitting there! I hadn't recognised her!
She'd put on a lot of weight. She was suffering.
As if some old unloved aunt had dropped by.
We kissed – once, twice – and made our way to the sea.
There was a man from Dakar on the beach
selling shells to put around the neck
as well as bangles and beads and silver bracelets
for the ankles and he thought I was Gloria's
husband – *marito* – and he asked me whether
I'd like some henna on my lady's body
and Gloria looked like a holy cow
covered with baubles and trinkets which swayed
and gleamed in the sun.
The man asked, Do you have children?
No, she said and he touched his heart (I'm sorry)
saying it was God's will and he told us
about the woman in Bangladesh whose womb
had been turned into a durian fruit.
You had to hold your nose as you drew near, he said
but the fruit of her womb was ecstasy.
(Some of this, I think, was lost in translation.)
We walked into the sea – the man with shells shouting
Great Fortune! Great Fortune! and you might have thought
Gloria was a boat as she pushed into the waves
with shells around her neck and bracelets around her
ankles and the henna smudged a little by the water,
and her feet were fused together and she shucked off

the cancer and the fibromyalgia and the weight,
and the girl who used to work at Principe Station
making platform change announcements
who for eighteen years was Lanfranco's mistress
became what the Italians call a *sirena*.
She looked at the shore, turning seawards,
swimming out of the Bay of Fables,
the white church tolling its bells across the town
and the coco bello man shouting *Coco bello!*
Coco bello! And that same morning a boy
from the village was killed on his motorbike.

Madonna dell' Orto

for Wendy

The vaporetto lurched and groaned.
The water rising, splashing the tables
of the café laid out on the front.
The Madonna dell' Orto.
The boatman lines up his boat.
People holding tight as they got off,
as they got on.
A cream motoscafo thumping past.
The lagoon that day was a garden under grey.
Rain coming.
The currents firing fish,
seabirds overhead,
the fruits of the sea,
the dead rising to the surface.
We saw Stravinsky and Brodsky,
we saw Diaghilev and Pound.
The water had given them their shape
their musculature, their purpose.
Half fish, half men.
Some had re-acquired their beards.
The lagoon reeled with the violins
of Olga Rudge.
Pound's jaws wide as a barracuda's:
snapping at the bream
snapping at the poles in the water
snapping at his reputation.

Quartet in C

The Cicada Armada fetched up in June:
a relentless hypnotic barrage.

Tutus

I came home to the Cicada Youth Orchestra
and I lay on the floor.
Our old mutt Bobby lay down beside me
panting.
When evening came
the fireflies, having put on their tutus, cavorted.

The CLA

Sectioned, I was sent to the Cicada Lunatic Asylum.
Doctor Coppola signed the papers.
His patients, he explained,
were beleaguered by obsessions.
Hence the cicadas which colonised the trees
in the great courtyard.
We were encouraged to adore them.
This was Doctor Coppola's radical way
of defying insanity, he was known across Europe.
It wasn't easy at first.
Spalgiando, si impara.
Practice makes perfect.
Imagine locked wards of relatively decent people
flapping their tongues.
Even the cicadas thought we were cicadas.
Saturdays
Doctor Coppola conducted his monomaniacal troupe
from the gazebo.
People came from Spoleto: wooden benches,
jugs of wine, hand-rolled cigarettes.

Bravissimo! Bravissimo!

Pimpinella

After ten years in the Cicada Lunatic Asylum
I was cured. Doctor Coppola signed the papers
and was almost brotherly. After a decade of cicadas
you may call me by my Christian name.
We are releasing you into Umbria – the lungs of Italy –
and he shook me by the hand. *Tante cose!*
I walked into the world with a healed mind
and when I felt hunger
Lanfranco the shepherd fed me on yesterday's bread.
His sheep had left him but he chanced upon them,
alive – yes – but they had suffered a change.
And peasant women who conversed with mushrooms
and an English-speaking woman called Daria
who'd long ago eaten fish with Doctor Jagger.
And a German who showed me his lederhosen.
I walked past medieval turrets, I saw castles
on the tops of mountains and heard tales
of the Knights Templar. I was never alone:
wild boar, red fox, deer, goats, bears shuffling down
from the Apennines and I delighted in the dragonfly
and the gecko and lovelorn donkeys
and mystical mules. Stray dogs befriended me
and I swam naked in the rivers, patrolled by kingfishers.
And lay under the lavendered blanket of the night
listening to wolves.
Somewhere swallows swooping over Trasimeno.
I faced the sun, the winds, the snow.
Strangers would give me a shed, a bed,
a plate of strangozzi, a suckling pig
and I came across villages wrecked by earthquakes

high on pimpinella, lentil flowers,
mustard flowers, poppies, legousia and fennel
and by the stream the lord prince, the Purple Heron.
I spent a week with a hermit. A month. A year.
Then I reached Bastardo
where I felt at home. They found me a house,
one up, one down, and because I spoke cicada fluently
I asked for a gentle symphony.
A black cat rubbed against my leg.
I had my own place – the Small House in Bastardo –
and I wrote to Doctor Coppola as he'd instructed,
without using his first name, I couldn't somehow,
even though I tried. Doctor Coppola, Doctor Coppola.
As promised he sent me a mental health worker
who was an olive-grower.
Eat these, he said, the olives of salvation
as if a green god were caressing my spleen
with the wing of a butterfly

Please Don't Bomb My Bed

My bed has several tricks up its sleeve.
(I bought it on the never-never, never-never.)
Sometimes it houses a small library
and a newspaper stand and a Portuguese café
with cinnamon and tarts.
Sometimes it becomes a German cabaret.
Happy to see you! Oh bleibe, bleibe stay . . .
I'm listening to Nina Simone:
here's my wedding ring. Goodbye old sleepy head
& remember darling – don't smoke in bed.
Some nights the duvet loses its shape.
Schopenhauer said life was a tin of prunes.
which was troublesome to open.
Sheet-washing's a crackerjack day – a carnival.
It's not always easy to sleep.
I listen to the Leningrad Symphony.
I listen to the World Service.
God have pity on us.

Please Don't Bomb My City

When my neighbour from India,
an IT specialist, moved in
I asked him what he thought of the city.
He waited a moment and said:
It's a shitty little city.
I was struck by his candour.
Nor did I think him wrong.
After six months he moved to Sydney.
His post flops into the hallway.
I'm still living in that city.
The shitty city.
My shitty shitty little city –

O Turkish barbers, Kurdish barbers.
The barbers from Kabul
who know the barbers from Seville.
The Pig 'N Whistle barbers
and the Black Sea Emporium barbers
and the ships' horns' barbers
and the foghorn barbers and the Pink Broadway Sauna
chock-a-block with barbers and sailors
(when the ships come in)
with their long tales and short sides
and the homeless barbers
and the Pound Shops and the pawn brokers
and the Albanian gangmasters
and the crackheads and the incapacitated.

The Luftwaffe bombed the city
for fifty nights.
When my friend from Stuttgart said
Can I see the beautiful part?
I said Which beautiful part?

Oh no, she said, oh no
I have asked the wrong question.
Margot, I said, that was a good question.

Please don't bomb my hips.
Please don't bomb my pelvis.
Please don't bomb my feet.
Please don't bomb my eyes.
Please don't bomb my kids.
Please don't bomb my concrete slab.
Please don't bomb the hospital.

Please don't bomb Dresden again.
Please don't bomb Hiroshima.
Please don't bomb the Viet Cong
Please don't bomb Baghdad,
Please don't bomb Aleppo.
Please don't bomb Slough.
Don't raise Mariupol to the ground.
God has abandoned Mariupol.
Leave Odessa in peace.
Please don't bomb my shitty shitty little city.

Please Don't Bomb My Head

There's a scar on my left cheek
& Monsieur Le Chin's sneaking off to Paris
to practice the accordion.
My mother gave me a comb for my hair.
I put the comb down somewhere.
I have an eye patch which I wear
during Lent. My teeth are yellowing –
There's no way out of the head.
Let's pray to God
it remains attached to my shoulders.

Please Don't Bomb My Black Dog

Black dog on the heath chases everything which moves.
I whistle plaintively. A black dot in the distance
thinking Whistle, whistle,
you can fucking whistle till the cows come home.

He's gone for days.
I know he'll slink back
smelling of pig shit and horse shit and cow shit
and every shit you can find on the heath
and every kind of shit beyond –
He stands outside the kitchen door howling in the dark.
Canine lamentation, cosmic shame.
Hunger.

I have done a great wrong, but I have come back.
I am filthy – shout at me – please don't beat me.
I'm not the beating kind. I say Bad, Bad Dog.

Bad, Bad Dog!

He whimpers, tries to lick my face.
I throw a bucket of water at him.
I get the dog towel
and have a go at scrubbing off the shit.
You'd better have some biscuits.
Looks a lot happier now
as if he's been to confession
and had his dog-sins wiped from the slate.

Upstairs is forbidden. He knows that.
He waits till I'm asleep and puts his foot
into the Rubicon and then he crosses the Rubicon.
He slides into the No Dog Zone,
nudges the bedroom door with his nose
and lies on the floor – waiting.
I listen to his scheming – too tired to speak.
He climbs onto the bed
and turns his back.

Edging closer.
He's hoping for some late-night spooning.
I will not spoon black dog.
I'm lying on my back
listening to the World Service.

I'm pretending to be asleep.
The dog thinks, *Hah, he's not snoring*
maybe light sleep, maybe dreaming in his sleep?
His heart's racing – he should learn to relax.

I heard him tell the cat, the one-eyed cat,
my snoring was like the storm of 1987.
I could have cut his biscuit rations for that.
Black dog's listening to the World Service.
He's yelping quietly and edging closer.
Project spooning on his mind.
He smells of pig, horse and rabbit
He smells of black dog.
I should have thrown another bucket over him.

I should have put him in the shed.
This reeking dog, this undisciplined dog,
this thrashable dog.
I curse him, I curse him again and again.
I smile in the dark.
I snore.

Please Don't Bomb My Ivory Tower

for David

I don't have one – as yet.
I don't have a piano.
I don't have tusks.
I have some teeth. I can bite.
If I could build a tower of ivory I would.
I'd sneak into a bombed house
and find a piano.
I'd take a hammer and smash it
to pieces

if it were not already in pieces –
I'd have some arrow slits put it
and get some Kalashnikovs.
I suspect my mother could use one
not to mention my sister
and the dog on the turret
would look to Sevastopol.

There would be many books
in many languages
including Herodotus and Thucydides
and Tolstoy and Henry James.
It's not unlike the Tower of Babel
in ivory.
And the most thumbed book in the library:

Dead Souls

Please Don't Bomb the Ghost of My Brother

He's riding a white horse.
I was going to say he was riding into the forest.
It's more like a wood, a large wood
with sycamore trees and silver birch
and if you look you can see a Weeping Willow.
There are deer in the undergrowth
watching carefully
and there are a lot of small animals.
He's talking to the horse and patting its neck.
There's no one else around
and the wood has a beguiling music.

The horse breaks into a canter.
Rabbits listen and twitch.
An oyster catcher flies overhead.
And coming into view a long-winged buzzard.

The horse slows and steps into the river –
He's a good horse, my brother's a good horseman.
Now they're getting out on the other side
where there are fewer trees.
The ghost of my brother finds a glade.
There must be a score of white horses.
There's sun light and there's a breeze.
The horses drink from the water.
And the ghosts, soldiers like my brother,
strip off and throw themselves into the lake.
Some lie on their backs.

My brother has slipped from view.
I bet you he's taken a big breath
kicked his legs and plunged down deep.
The horses stand under a tree.
My brother's horse is whinnying.

Beyond

Wake up Poseidon. You've been asleep too long.
Your beard's full of barnacles and your horse needs hoof care.

Earth Shaker stretches and opens wide, in glides stargazer –
breakfast, *nice*. Blue water, blue earth, a spectral blueprint.
It's already happened, or it hasn't, or it will, somewhere else, beyond.

Poseidon walks through the palace, happy now, and pronged.
He's going on a space trip.
He's all sketch book and doodle and Euclidian squib.
He's all pillar and plinth and rocket and whalebone.
Lord of the Nymphs. Astronauts love him. The scientists cheer.

Tiresias, you can come out from behind that divan, he says.
I've decided you're coming with me.
You can answer the phone. You can order soft furnishings.

Silk, organza, rhapsodize the beyond, phantasmic bonanza.
We'll travel in style – you, me and the horse – a ménage a trois.
We'll speak Greek on a planet which hasn't been given a name.
We'll ride out at dawn, bathe in a stream, chill in our space boudoir.

The El Supremo

I knew he wasn't dead.
There'd been no confirmed sightings
since the drowning but we waited, the children waited.
For a while mother set a plate at the table –
She took up drinking. She was good at it.
People lose their memories, we've read the books.
They're in a restaurant, smoking.
They're drinking gin and tonic, the sky is blue.
Some days they almost feel new.

You can't relinquish a body never found.
Objects gone from the flat in Jakarta.
There was talk of a Chinese girlfriend.
She didn't have the heart to hang around.
Some days I like to think of her.
Let's call her Lizzy Fung.
My brother's girl – she disappeared into the world.
A songbird.

You might live quietly in Argentina,
the Philippines – Montana – anywhere.
Make ends meet.

My brother's body broken.

Driftwood.

A cygnet ring –

Palpable.

A sea change.

No Lazarus.

Yet.

You were forty-seven, frozen at forty-seven.
Heroic age.
More rounds of the track.
Not some rackety Volvo – things were looking up!

My brother would drive a sports car.
There would be parties, music.
His children would love him, indulge him, rattle him.
Sooner or later grandchildren.
He would be generous. He was always generous.
I, the younger older brother, at sixty.
Getting younger every day, diminished.

I have a photograph – my brother's ten.
Reeking of boarding school.
All life ahead.
My older brother – the El Supremo.
His was the room at the top of the stairs.

I saw him on the Circle Line.
I saw him in Liguria coming out of the sea,
his hair long.
The sky was full of songbirds.

I saw him in Honk Kong, Singapore, Jakarta –
I was there to watch Lizzy flying over the house.
I saw my brother walking out,
the El Supremo – with that Steely Dan T-Shirt.
The words were pouring out of his mouth:

While the dead people sleep

in the shade of the light –

While the dead people sleep

all the stars come out at night.

I saw two birds flying over the house

The Magnificence of Death

We could hear the hooves of the Mongols.
Our walled city was hanging fruit, hanging low.
I could see my head on a pole –
Our bowmen had slipped away in the night.

We could kneel down and beg mercy and then
have our heads cut off or we could have our heads
cut off without the bother of kneeling down.

What say you?

There was some opium left. I'll have that.
The beetroot merchant had fled too.
The smartest thing he'd ever done.

We have no cannon ball, the captain said.
We have beets the size of giants' gonads.
Let's boil them and make a pool of blood.

And when the Mongols climb the ramparts
we'll let the beet rain down upon them.

Is that some kind of joke captain?

The reason I'm standing here
and you're standing there
is because I passed the Imperial Exams.
I read Li Po's treatise on warfare,
at least most of it.

Do you have a better idea?

I rather liked peeling the beets
even as the hooves got nearer
occasionally having a bite,
not bad, not great either.

Before long we could see the Mongol flags.
Water ran down our soldiers' legs
even as we cracked jokes to keep our spirits up.
Have you heard the one about the Mongol
and the Archbishop of Budapest?

My hands were bloodied like a murderer's.
No one could say we lived dull lives.

And the musicians reached for instruments
and played a piece long before its time
that would be copied by some doleful goth
a name like Beet-Hosan many years hence
called Speaking unto Nations.
If only we could speak to the Mongols
and ask them to go away.

I don't know how or why I know this
or what prompted the court musicians to refrain
from their usual din but thank God they did.
A moment of genius, a moment of terror.

By now the Mongols were catapulting
the severed heads of concubines.

I was in a reverie:
as fragrant as the Emperor's Vale of Stars.

Wet-cheeked I remembered afternoons
of gentle spooning followed by
the choicest parts of armadillo.
Sweet faraway non-Mongolian days!

Oi soldier, concentrate –
Pierced by arrows
my head not yet mounted on a pole
(getting there . . .)
we let them have it.

SS Nevasa

A pair of maroon-coloured boots
with liquorice laces
in the corner
waiting for mother's feet

which are in the bed, with the rest of her.
She's ninety-four, she has a fever.
She's coughing, breathless.
We got the doctor out
driving through the snow,
a pair of buzzards overhead.

Antibiotics, soup.
Cough, cough, cough.
The maroon-coloured boots
quiet in the corner.

More coughing, more soup.
More medicine. *More.*
A pair of buzzards on the heath.

She's propped up now,
pillows behind her back
It was 1958, she says.
Southampton.
Aboard the SS Nevasa.
A troopship. Four weeks
before we reached Singapore.

My sister's five years old,
my brother two.

There's a military band on the SS Nevasa.
There's silver service.
Drinks with the captain
long dresses and dinner jackets
and soldiers exercising on the deck.
There isn't a cot for my two-year old brother.

My brother isn't used to a life-sized bed.
The possibilities are endless.
Had to have eyes
at the back of your head
my mother says.

They're sailing through the Suez Canal.
Camels, Egyptian soldiers.
The sun's setting on the Empire.

We had to keep an eye on him, my mother says.

The Red Sea was a blaze of heat.
No air conditioning.
When your brother was asleep
I'd open the door.

The only two-year-old on the ship.
Cot-less.

Twenty-four hours in the port of Aden.
Bumboats to and fro.
Then we were in the Indian Ocean.
The heat was overwhelming.
They gave us salt tablets.
PT instructors on the deck.
Firing practice at the stern.
Soldiers firing into the beyond.

Mother wakes in the night.
My brother's shouting *Mummy! Mummy!*
He's slipping through the passageways,
climbing onto the upper deck,
the lower deck.
slipping into the bowels.
Somewhere there's a military band.
The captain has another gin.
Sharks trailing the ship.

Mummy! Mummy!

Mother wakes in the night.
Adrenaline hits her like an arrow.
She's out of bed, lacing up the boots.
Not ideal for the Indian Ocean.
No time to worry about that.

She's almost running through the ship.
She thinks she can hear

the Italian opera singer
singing to the stars.

Mummy! Mummy!

One version of the story tells us
he fell into a cleaner's bucket,
bottom first, and that was that,
the end of his adventures,
at least for now.

And when she finds him in the night
she's going to wallop him.
Then hold him tight, tight, tight.

The Committal

IM: Steadman Stephen Thompson (1966–2022), Writer

They dug a deep hole and the brothers filled it
with the help of a dumper truck
which dropped the earth next to the grave.
It was hot and the brothers wiped themselves
with towels and took a little rum
to give themselves heft, and a great aunt
– veiled – read aloud from her psalm book even though
Jimmy Cliff's Many Rivers to Cross was playing on a stereo.
Her voice was pure, and once into her stride she sang
Amazing Grace, how sweet the sound that saved a wretch like me.
And the brothers smoked weed to stay in the spirit groove.
It took more than an hour to fill the hole.
It was an act of love, it was an act of suffering.
The black mourners were dressed in black:
top hats, Rasta caps, suits, some as sharp as
the Tonton Macoutes: soldiers of the rugged cross,
soldiers of a higher power.

It has pleased Almighty God to take him from this world.
We therefore commit his body to the ground,
earth to earth, ashes to ashes, dust to dust.
I am the resurrection and the life to come.
The words rolled off the vicar's tongue.

Kass – Stephen's white 'missus' – at the graveside
taken in by the Jamaican Brotherhood, the Jamaican Sisterhood.
Her grief encircled.
As the flowers were placed on the grave
'To know him was to love him'

I saw Stephen slipping through the gravestones
towards the wood. He was moving fast
clutching *Love in the Time of Cholera*.

He wasn't going to lie down in the London Cemetery.
Some of him would lie down, some would get the hell out:
relax a while, a flight to Athens, the boat to Ithaca.

He's slipping into mythical water, washing off the dust.
They're grilling fish on the beach.

Oh Stephen, great writer, dear friend:
finish that book on Marcus Garvey.
There's always a beginning, there's never an end

Acknowledgments

Several of these poems have appeared in *Poetry Review, Poetry London, Spectator, Bad Lilies, Anthropocene, Exacting Clam* (USA), *Ink, Sweat and Tears* and the NAWE Journal *Writing in Education*. 'Beyond' was a response to Juliette Mahieux Bartoli's 'Extrasolar', a cyanotype on organza. The collaboration was part of 'A Fine Day for Seeing' (Ten Poets, Ten Artists), an exhibition held at Southwark Park Galleries in London from 28 July to 29 August 2021, curated by Paul Carey-Kent and Dr Tamar Yoseloff.

Special thanks to colleagues and poet friends including Robyn Bolam and Stephen Duncan and Wendy Falla; and thanks to the editors of *Exacting Clam* for their generous support. Madeleine and Charles have provided food and water and a bed in Shepherd's Bush on many occasions; thank you for that! It was nice to be part of The Glue Factory, David Collard's weekly online gathering. With much fondness and sadness I remember my friend and colleague Stephen Thompson who died in 2022.

This book has been typeset by
SALT PUBLISHING LIMITED
using Sabon, a font designed by Jan Tschichold
for the D. Stempel AG, Linotype and Monotype Foundries.
It is manufactured using Holmen Book Cream 70gsm,
a Forest Stewardship Council™ certified paper from the
Hallsta Paper Mill in Sweden. It was printed and bound
by Clays Limited in Bungay, Suffolk, Great Britain.

CROMER
GREAT BRITAIN
MMXXIII